Praise

'Your Money Your Impact is a must-read book given it's been written by a gifted and conscientious financial planner who shares her insights around the problems we're experiencing with the financial services industry and how to fix them. Finding your way forward amidst the maze of financial products and services requires an experienced guide who is dedicated and committed to your journey and your outcomes. A rare and much-needed reliable source of information to further your impact on your life for you, your family and your community.'

— **Betty-Anne Howard** CFP® MFA-P
   CLU CHS CEA

Your
Money
Your
Impact

Connect with your values
and design a financial plan that
leaves a lasting legacy

Lynn L Whetham CFP®

Rethink

First published in Great Britain in 2023
by Rethink Press (www.rethinkpress.com)

© Copyright Lynn Whetham

All rights reserved. No part of this publication may be reproduced, stored in or introduced into a retrieval system, or transmitted, in any form, or by any means (electronic, mechanical, photocopying, recording or otherwise) without the prior written permission of the publisher.

The right of Lynn Whetham to be identified as the author of this work has been asserted by her in accordance with the Copyright, Designs and Patents Act 1988.

This book is sold subject to the condition that it shall not, by way of trade or otherwise, be lent, resold, hired out, or otherwise circulated without the publisher's prior consent in any form of binding or cover other than that in which it is published and without a similar condition including this condition being imposed on the subsequent purchaser.

Cover image © Brooklane Creative Ltd

Disclaimer
The content of this book is for information only. You should undertake your own research and analysis, and take independent financial advice from a professional, before making any decisions or investments, based on your personal circumstances. Neither Rethink Press nor the author can be held liable in respect of any damage, expense, other loss or adverse effects you may suffer as a consequence of relying on the information provided in this book.

This book is dedicated to all the kind souls who want to leave the world a better place.

Contents

Introduction   **1**

   Planning for a rainy day   6

1 Mindful Money Management   **11**

   Spending   14

   Investing   21

   Donating   26

   Legacy   30

   Summary   32

2 Ways In Which The Financial Planning Industry Is Failing You   **35**

   Stealing your peace of mind   36

   Ignoring your values   37

   Not explaining all your options   40

   Silos   41

	Creating unnecessary complexity	43
	Ignoring you in your growth stages	45
	Failing to provide value	46
	Summary	47
3	**Seven Steps To A Legacy Of Love**	**49**
	Summary	60
4	**An Impactful Estate Plan**	**61**
	Purpose	64
	Personal history	67
	Your 'why'	69
	The right team and leadership	71
	A work in progress	75
	Summary	76
5	**Choice**	**79**
	As simple as ABC	80
	A: Already decided	81
	B: Better for your family	81
	C: Consider your legacy	82
	Special needs	86
	Summary	88

6 Mindful Communication	**89**
Storytelling	91
Teaching about giving	96
Summary	98
Conclusion	**99**
Contribution by design	100
Resources	**105**
Further reading	105
Core values exercise	106
Acknowledgements	**113**
The Author	**115**

Introduction

This is a book about you, your family and your impact on the world. It will help you to identify the values you hold dear and explore ways to uphold your principles and address your ideals. It's about the message you want to send to your loved ones, the beliefs you want to display and the mark you want to make on your community – whether that is local, regional or international.

Since 1995, I have been helping socially conscious people like you make values-based investment and philanthropic decisions that enable you to make a far greater impact than you might have thought possible. Although my formal training has taken place over the course of over twenty-five years (and counting) as I've honed my trade, it is what I have learned from the people I have worked with that informs the content of this book. While I've learned a great deal from reading and formal studies, I am even more indebted to the people whose stories I will share with you here.

You will also hear from some of the thought leaders who have influenced me in my journey. Many of these brilliant and committed people have become dear friends after sharing their stories on my radio show, Mindful Money Management. Not all of the people you will meet in this book are scholars or experts. Some are ordinary people, people like you, who have chosen to make a commitment in their financial life to seek a better world.

Over the course of my career in financial services, I have met many thoughtful and passionate people who thought they had no meaningful way to control their legacy. Their heart was in the right place but they never thought their wallet, or their estate, could reflect that.

That is why I created the Mindful Money Management process – to empower people to make conscious decisions when it comes to their money. Over the course of this book, I will show you how. As author of *Retire Abundantly* and host of the Mindful Money Management radio show, I have motivated thousands around the world to take the first step, which is understanding and believing you can make a difference and have an impact well beyond your wildest dreams.

By helping people like you to identify and multiply your influence, my team and I have shown Canadians and other concerned citizens around the world how to fulfill their powerful purpose – at every stage of life. My motto is, 'We are happiest when we protect and communicate our values through the way we spend, invest and donate.'

Did you watch the news last night? Did you see examples of people living up to exceptional values, or stories about people you feel missed the mark? Do you ever feel that the world is spiralling out of control? Do you wish that you could have a greater influence? Do you feel that efforts to affect change are futile? Do you feel powerless to make any impact on the world?

The only way to see positive change is to make positive choices. Lots of people talk about their rights; not nearly so many talk about their obligations. With obligations come inspiring, meaningful opportunities. If you've picked up this book, it's likely because you want to have a powerful and positive impact. You want to influence the world for good and generate positive change. You want to take control because you feel a responsibility to help your neighbour, however you define your neighbourhood. If, like me, you want to believe, to *know*, that at the end of your life you can say that you lived a life with purpose, from both a personal and a financial point of view, this book is for you.

We live in a complex world. This is especially true when it comes to finances. Opinions abound. Most of those opinions seek to separate financial wellbeing from social commitment. That doesn't have to be the case. The overwhelming abundance of views, advice and approaches may leave you applying strategies that do not align with your objectives and perhaps even conflict with your values. Many in the financial services industry will lead you to believe that this is 'just how it is'. In this book, I will show you that this does not have to be the case. Some of the problem lies in the things they don't tell you. Issues you are not aware of can inflict serious harm if left unchecked. Without a sense of purpose, you can end up lacking direction and clarity about what you want to accomplish.

There are barriers in the financial planning industry that may limit your options. For one, it's difficult to find the information you need; and finding the expertise needed to utilize the information you do uncover can be even more challenging. Creative solutions may not be readily available, but rest assured, they are out there – I'll show you how to find them.

I see so many people who leave their financial future to fate because they cannot see another way. Maybe you share the sense that it's too much work to take control; it's easier to give it up. But traditional planning may set you up to fail. This failure can come in many forms. It may be expressed in the net worth you are able (or not) to attain or hold onto. Or it may be reflected in neglecting heartfelt goals and purposes simply because you are unaware of the creative solutions out there that could enable you to achieve them. Maintaining a sole focus on building net worth neglects the personal and social dimensions of wealth and will likely leave you unmotivated and unfulfilled. It can prevent you from experiencing a life of meaning and, hence, of joy.

I am dedicated to empowering socially conscious individuals like you to manage your financial resources for the benefit of yourself, your family and your community. I want to help you make conscious decisions, knowing that each aspect of your financial plan takes you closer to your desired outcome. I want you to have confidence to face the future making choices that reflect your dreams and values and to experience the joy that comes from knowing that your unique purpose will be fulfilled, and your wealth will have an impact.

Planning for a rainy day

My preferred leisure activity is trail riding on horseback. I like nothing better than loading up a horse or two in the trailer and joining a friend for a weekend of camping and riding the trails. One of my favourite places to ride is Ganaraska Forest – 11,000 acres of pure bliss. This is where I first started trail riding in 2012. Back then, I didn't venture out without one of the more experienced riders as a guide – some of them have been riding horse trails for twenty-five years – because it's easy to lose your sense of direction on the twisting and turning trails that run through Ganaraska.

Over time, my confidence grew and my need for a guide slipped away. A couple of years ago, my friend Carrie and I headed out on our own. I went out on Winchester and Carrie took my other horse, Monty. We packed a lunch. We had a map, a GPS and a compass. Everything we could possibly need, right?

Our plan was to ride until lunch, then sit down and plan our path back to camp. We were having the greatest time, exploring a ridge I had never been on before, and then it happened – the clouds opened up and a cold September rain began to pelt down on us. It all happened so fast. I pulled out my map and it quickly disintegrated in my hands. The screen on my GPS faded to black – it had taken in moisture. Now what? Thanks to Carrie's compass, we got ourselves headed in the right direction and, fortunately, we came across a spot that I recognized. I had been there for the first time just the day before. It was at the bottom of a big hill that we call 'the lookout'. I had visited the lookout itself many times, though this side was new to me, but as soon as we climbed up the hill, I knew the path back to camp.

Like a compass in a storm, the greatest value you'll get from your written financial plan won't be when the skies are sunny, though it still helps in these times too. Times of change are excellent times to assess your financial situation. Starting school, graduation, marriage, retirement – these are all positive life changes, and your plan can give valuable guidance. But the greatest value will come when the skies open, when you get dumped on and life brings unexpected challenges: job loss, poor health, death, divorce. A comprehensive written financial plan will help you to make good decisions in the rough times and keep you on track to accomplish your goals.

As I sit down to write this book, we are witnessing a series of financial storms that no one would have believed possible just a few years back. In the summer of 2022, we are recovering from the COVID-19 crisis that brought unimaginable distress – physical, mental and financial. And we are now months into a horrific war in Ukraine and seeing inflationary economic conditions not witnessed in a generation. In such conditions, we need a financial plan that will help us weather even the most torrential of downpours.

This book will be your guide. It will teach you how you can express your values throughout your lifetime in the way you spend, invest and donate your money. You will discover little-known estate strategies that enable you to redirect tax money to the causes you care about. You will learn how barriers in the financial planning industry keep you in the dark about your options.

In this book, I will share the Mindful Money Management lifetime process: Seven Steps to a Legacy of Love. This will enable you to design a high-impact financial legacy that will support generations to come. Be sure it is you who designs your contribution to your family and community – it's far too important to leave to chance.

Let's get started.

1
Mindful Money Management

I get upset when I hear people say that making a profit comes at the expense of maintaining values. That making money and doing good are mutually exclusive and we must choose between profit and our values. That proposition doesn't sit well with me; it's a false choice.

I want to show you that you can have both – a decent rate of return and a clear conscience. You can do well *and* do good. It might take some extra thought and consideration, but you can do it. I have seen it happen for clients who have found peace of mind with their money and their goals. Let's be clear. To truly succeed, profit and values *must* go together. Based on that conviction, I developed and grew the Mindful Money Management program.

To enable you to understand how Mindful Money Management can help put your financial house in order, I want to share a simple story with you that I think you'll be able to relate to.

One Saturday morning, I got up early for Pilates. I was dressed in my exercise clothes, ready to go to class, work up a sweat, get all limber and start my weekend off on the right note. I got in my car and the next thing I knew, I was at my office. How did that happen? I was just thinking about other stuff. In my head was a list of 'must dos', 'need to dos' and 'want to dos' and then… I was at my office. I wasn't consciously thinking about where I was going, so I ended up somewhere else.

The same thing can happen when you are not conscious about your finances. Other stuff gets in the way and your money doesn't receive the attention it deserves. Your progress toward your goals suffers and you risk missing the mark. You can be mindful of the way you spend your money every day, and mindful of how you invest for the future. You can be mindful in the way you donate. As you make these choices, you can be mindful of your values.

With every choice you make, every penny you spend, invest and donate, you cast a vote. So why not vote for profit with values?

This might initially sound overwhelming. 'I have to make mindful choices every time I buy something? I thought this book was about investing. I understand that I should only donate to things I believe in, but the rest of it? Come on…!'

If you're struggling to know where to begin, think about it this way. When you start something like a Pilates program (or a meditation practice – mindfulness, anyone?) it can feel overwhelming, packed full of new ideas and jargon. Over time, though, it gets easier and becomes second nature. To put your mind at ease, the program I have developed isn't anywhere near as difficult as Pilates or meditation.

Spending

First, let's talk about spending. We spend money every day. Most of the time, we do it without much conscious thought. When you buy things, you can be mindful of the companies you are supporting. This is probably one of the best examples of where it's worth spending time doing some research, finding out what companies are doing things and making choices that you can support – and those that are doing things you disagree with.

Let's make something clear upfront: we're all human. There will be times when, despite your best intentions, you buy things and use companies that fall outside of your mindfulness framework. It will happen. You can learn from it and move on. It's a bit like grabbing a sugary snack when you're trying to be healthy – you won't get it right all the time. I've been there and done that.

Over time, though, you'll decide and learn what you are comfortable with and what sets alarm bells ringing. Maybe you even do that already. Let me give you an example of a purchase I made a conscious decision about, after looking at the evidence in front of me. The trigger was an item on my seventeen-year-old grandson's Christmas list, a shirt from a particular brand of clothing. It sounded simple enough and, being the doting grandmother that I am, I went to the mall, located the right store and found the shirt. All I had to do next was take the shirt to the register, buy it, take it home, wrap it up and put it under the tree. But I couldn't do it. The slogan on the front of the shirt read: 'Cocaine and caviar'. I had a horrible sinking feeling in the pit of my stomach. Every cell in my body was reacting negatively to those words. I wanted my grandson to have the shirt he had asked for, but I could never buy a shirt with that slogan on it.

Both those words symbolize concepts, worldviews, that I find repulsive. I was not going to support a company (through my purchase) that promoted ideas I thought were revolting. It seemed that this company was telling young people that cocaine would somehow lead to a lifestyle that includes caviar. The word 'caviar' alone calls to mind an extravagance that doesn't reflect my values – values that I suspect (or at least, I hope) my grandson shares.

Fortunately, there was another brand with similar style shirts that didn't glorify cocaine or caviar, so I spent my money on one of those instead and was pleased when it became my grandson's favourite. I used my money to vote for my values, just by buying a different brand of shirt. That's practising Mindful Money Management. It can be that simple, or it can be more involved. That's for you to decide.

There's a lot of talk about buying Canadian and buying local. That's important. You might also consider the conditions of the workers where the product is made and the effect of your purchase on the wider economy, on our neighbours' jobs and on the environment. When you make a decision based on these kinds of considerations, you are practising Mindful Money Management.

As you learn about and begin to practice Mindful Money Management, you will see that there are two kinds of purchasing decisions you make: the things you decide *not* to purchase because they upset, disturb or offend you (like shirts that read 'Cocaine and caviar'); and the things you decide to purchase because you actively support them or the person/company selling them. Anyone for a Girl Guide cookie?

As you work through this program you will need to make these kinds of decisions again and again. 'Do I or don't I buy this, based on my values and how they are reflected (or not) in this item/service?' This applies equally to your investment decisions and your charitable donations. Thinking this way means you'll be making positive decisions about where to spend and where to withhold your money, every step of the way.

There will be times when there is no clear choice. That's OK. Life has grey areas.

MAKING POSITIVE CHOICES – PAMELA D'ETTORRE

I want to share with you an example of a positive purchase choice I made years ago and that I still practice today.

The episode of the Mindful Money Management radio show that has had the greatest impact on me was one in which I had a conversation with Pamela D'Ettorre about ethics in the fashion industry. Pamela had been involved in the industry for over thirty-five years and what she shared with me in the hour I spent with her changed the way I shop for clothes, when I wash my clothes and even *how* I wash my clothes.

We talked about fast fashion and what is involved in producing the fibres that are used to make our clothes. We looked at the industry's environmental impact and how the people who produce these clothes and the things that go into them are treated.

Pamela pointed out that cotton needs five times more water to grow than hemp. She talked about the pesticides and chemicals used to grow cotton and to dye fabrics. She explained about 'recycling' clothes and, when they are ultimately thrown away as garbage, how long they take to decompose. We talked about the complete life cycle of every shirt you have in your drawers.

'Traditional cotton requires a great deal of chemical intervention to grow, and we should ensure that the people who are working in the fields have proper coverage, ventilation, masks and gloves, so that when they are spraying, they aren't inhaling these chemicals because often they are highly carcinogenic and workers can be poisoned,' Pamela explained.

'Some people are very sensitive to these chemicals and can only wear clothes that haven't been in contact with them. Really, we're talking about the environment and about all the people who have had to handle these chemicals all the way through the process.'

As a result of this conversation, in 2020, I committed to not buying any more clothes of any kind. I had plenty already in my wardrobe. I think it was hearing Pamela talk about blue jeans that led me to make that pledge. She said that there are seven pairs of jeans out there for every person on the planet. Obviously, some people have none and others many more, but she highlighted this statistic to make a point about society's 'hoarding mentality'. If there are dozens of pairs of jeans in your closet, how can you possibly wear, or need, all of them? This is just hoarding resources when we don't need to.

'In reality, I have taken all that intrinsic energy from growing the cotton, shipping the cotton to a factory, dyeing it, twisting it into yarns, weaving it into fabric, cutting it into pants and shipping it to a store, and hoarded it in my closet,' she told me.

If we have the means to buy what we want, we have no financial constraints stopping us from engaging in this kind of hoarding. We can also throw this stuff out if we want to, without a second thought.

'Now we have second-hand stores and consignment stores, where we can say, "I'm done with this, you can have it," and we can feel good about donating our discarded clothing to charity. We must ask ourselves: what hole are we filling by purchasing so much?'

Before the Industrial Revolution, making textiles was time-consuming and expensive, and clothes were often handed down from one generation to the next. I think the only example of that we still see is when a bride wears their mother's wedding dress – and most people now think that tradition is quaint. And when was the last time you heard of a groom wearing their father's suit?

'Now we can make thousands of metres of fabric per minute. The speed at which we can make textiles now makes them disposable because we can replace them so easily,' Pamela explained.

She went on to tell me that over 10 million tons of clothing go to landfill every year in North America; 95% of those clothes could be reused or recycled, or simply kept in your closet and not replaced.

'It's heart-breaking,' Pamela concluded.[1]

---

1   L Whetham, 'Ethics and the fashion industry: Guest Pamela D'Ettorre', Stepright with Lynn (rebranded Mindful Money Management) (25 March 2015), www.soundcloud.com/mindfulmoneymanagement/ethics-and-the-fashion-industry-with-guest-pamela-dettorre, accessed 12 March 2022

When we have purchasing power, we have choices to make; every choice, every purchase that we make, casts a vote for our values. Consider plastics and packaging, for example. You have a choice here. There are no-waste dry goods stores where you can bring your own bag to buy almonds, raisins or paprika, your health and beauty products too.

What about electronics? It's relatively easy to find and purchase good quality, durable clothing that we won't need to replace, or to just keep the clothes you already have in your wardrobe. But no one wants to get trapped with a vintage cell phone. It's probably the most expensive device that most of us own, and there are always new options and system updates that press us to get the latest technology. On top of that, these devices use rare metals and minerals that need to be found and then mined. The environmental and humanitarian costs of this relentless replacing and upgrading are scary to think about.

Investing

When we invest money, we can again be mindful of the companies we support. There's a growing movement of those seeking to invest in socially responsible companies that strive to not only make money but also have a positive impact on the world. These are companies pursuing a win/win situation, hoping to benefit the business owners, shareholders, employees and the community. Increasingly, companies are entering the market that create profit with purpose, that have strong moral values and try to minimize their environmental impact.

All investors look to purchase stocks of profitable companies – companies that make money. Socially responsible investing is the process of making investment decisions based on both traditional financial analysis plus an evaluation of a company's performance on environmental, social and governance factors. This extra level of research gives fund managers a fuller picture of each company. It's not something new or different; it's an extension of established and sound investment practice. A socially responsible investment fund will look for profitable companies that also reflect the values the fund (and its investors) seeks to uphold and support.

Terms you need to know

Environmental, Social and Governance (ESG)

Perhaps you have already heard of ESG. It's getting an increasing amount of attention as the world becomes more aware of the impact of our actions and of business on the planet and on our fellow citizens. The term ESG is now universally used to define ethical investment choices. But what exactly does it mean?'

In the simplest terms, ESG stands for environmental, social and governance – an investor can evaluate a company on their practices in these three categories. ESG is a way to enhance traditional financial analysis, to identify risks and opportunities beyond what a standard evaluation would look for. The main concern of ESG investing is still financial performance, but with an overlay of social consciousness.

According to Hank Smith of The Haverford Trust Company, 'There's a misconception out there that you need to be willing to give up returns in order to invest responsibly but a growing body of research shows that ESG actually helps mitigate risk.'[2]

Socially responsible investing (SRI)

Socially responsible investment goes even further than ESG, though it is generally considered to have come before it. While ESG has been around since the 1960s, SRI has its roots in movements to abolish slavery, to secure the vote for women and to overthrow apartheid.[3]

SRI involves actively eliminating or selecting investment opportunities in accordance with ethical guidelines decided on by individual investors. These guidelines can be motivated by personal beliefs, religion, or political convictions. SRI does not use ESG analysis to make investment decisions; instead, it uses ESG factors to apply negative or positive lenses to the investment universe and screen certain things in or out of consideration. In the loosest terms,

---

2 E Napoletano and B Curry, 'Environmental, social and governance: What is ESG investing?', *Forbes* (24 February 2022), www.forbes.com/advisor/investing/esg-investing, accessed 26 November 2022

3 Corporate Finance Institute Team, 'Socially Responsible Investment (SRI)', CFI (13 October 2022), https://corporatefinanceinstitute.com/resources/esg/socially-responsible-investment-sri, accessed 6 December 2022

where ESG is analytical and mathematical, SRI is more feeling.

The following are some possible negative affiliations that SRI might screen for:

- Addictive substances such as alcohol and/or tobacco
- Gambling
- Production of firearms and weapons
- Terrorism
- Violations of human rights and labour laws
- Environmental damage

Some people criticize SRI and ESG on the basis of screening more for negative factors than for positive ones. I'll talk about positive SRI screens when I get into impact investing, but as my earlier story about the shirt showed, it is often easier to figure out what you want to stay away from. Even so, as you will remember, in the end, I found a positive alternative.

Socially responsible investing is a way for investors to make a profit and respect their principles. The goal is to make returns without compromising your conscience.

Impact investing

Impact investing goes further still, making positive (non-financial) outcomes the most important focus. In this kind of investing, businesses and companies are chosen for the positive impact they are having, or intend to have, on society or the environment.

When investors choose to base their investment choices on their values, they are acting in accordance with the principles of my Mindful Money Management program. As a shareholder, you can influence the companies you invest in to reflect your values.

Donating

When we donate money, we should be mindful of the causes we support. How often are you asked to give money to a cause? How frequently do you have people ringing your doorbell? How many times is your dinner interrupted by a phone call? When was the last time you weren't asked to make a donation at the checkout?

I like to encourage kids to put themselves out there to help someone else. It takes a lot for a young person to knock on a door and ask for support for the cause they've chosen, so I've made a mindful decision that when kids ask, I will give. I like it when they can talk about the cause that they're supporting. I think it's good for them to give their time in this way, so I choose to support them when they do.

But I used to give every time the phone rang. Sometimes, it felt like it was solely my responsibility to send every child in the city to the circus. And thank goodness I answered the phone the next time because it seemed that the police force was depending on me to single-handedly finance their latest campaign. That was how it was for me until I worked through the Mindful Money Management program for myself. I still donate to charity, but as and when I choose, after conducting thorough research. And I never get conned because I can tell the difference between genuine charitable organizations and businesses using guilt to manipulate people into giving money.

When you are asked to give money at a store checkout, that is a charity that they have chosen, not you. You haven't had a chance to give it any thought. You think you are helping but when you are mindful, you may realize that your money could do more good (and on your terms, aligned with your values) elsewhere. Think about your giving and be sure you use it to cast a vote for what is important to you.

Mindful Money Management has brought me together with people who have gone on to become deeply engaged in causes that they are passionate about and that give their lives new meaning. These people give by applying themselves to a cause. Would you not prefer to channel your donation to a cause that you feel a deep connection to? What if you could find a charitable organization whose goals were aligned with your purpose, that you were excited to get involved with whenever there was a need and you were asked to help? A meaningful gift flows from the giver to the receiver but it touches both.

MINDFUL GIVING – ANNE MACKAY

My friend Anne MacKay has worked for over twenty-five years in the non-profit sector and often helps people decide on the best charity for them to support. When I interviewed Anne for the Mindful Money Management radio show, she said: 'Charitable giving is another way people can vote – you really want to honour that intention. Is this the right charity to accomplish what they want to see happen in the community? Seeing people who are so excited about their gifts that they get teary – that's amazing.'

One of the clients Anne worked with was a very health-focused person who wanted to support a charity with her small business. 'We talked about food banks and issues around health. We looked at how she wanted to be involved. Did she want to just write a cheque?'

What Anne's client wanted was a partnership where she could involve her clients if they were interested. She also wanted to get involved as a volunteer. 'So we started looking across the community at organizations that might be able to accommodate her. It was a little like Goldilocks,' Anne explained. 'Somewhere would be just a little too "this", another was a little too "that", but, we finally found an organization for her. Not only was she able to give to an organization that mattered to her, but they also brought her in as a volunteer and she has since joined their board. She's found a whole new community that has meaning and learning to share with her, so her life got bigger. I think she would be the first to say that, and she really feels like she's getting more than she's giving. That's a wonderful experience to watch.'[4]

Legacy

Sometimes, our choices can be out of alignment with our values without us even being aware of it. But as we learn more about the consequences of our decisions we can choose to do better. There is a satisfaction that comes when choices and values are aligned. What makes some people even happier is learning they can continue to make a difference to the causes they love after they die, that their gift can live on. Their values become their legacy.

Whether you want to leave money to your spouse, your kids, your favourite charity, or your cat, you can show who and what you value, and share this with your loved ones, by being mindful.

---

4 L Whetham, 'Make your giving matter to you: Guest Anne MacKay', Stepright with Lynn (rebranded Mindful Money Management) (23 April 2014), https://soundcloud.com/mindfulmoneymanagement/make-your-giving-matter-to-you-with-anne-mackay-1, accessed 12 March 2022

When Joe walked into my office, he thought he knew what would happen when he died. He didn't believe he had much, and it would just go to his family. Joe worked as a custodian at a school near his home. He had a great relationship with the staff and students. As he walked to work each day, he passed a neighbourhood park. When we explored what Joe wanted his money to do, we determined that he really wanted to see a splash pad in that park. When we applied Mindful Money Management, we found that Joe could finance that project and leave more for his family and much less to the government. All it took was a repositioning of assets. The gift he made to charity showed his family that giving was important to him. He used his money to vote for his values.

Toronto philanthropist and CEO of The Donor Motivation Program®, Keith Thomson, says that in Canada most people do not consider their legacy. Keith illustrates the difference between traditional estate planning and values-based planning by asking people if they know their great grandmother's name. 'The responses I receive to this question most effectively demonstrate the difference between traditional estate planning, with its focus primarily on the money, and a more effective approach to planning which is driven by life's most important treasures: relationships and values,' he explains. Keith goes on to reveal that about two-thirds of people can't remember their great grandmother's name. The idea that his own great grandchildren might be among them didn't sit well with him. 'It was then that I decided my life must reflect some sort of personal legacy, that would continue to make a positive impact long after I was gone while, at the same time, communicate to future generations the values that had been most meaningful to me.'[5]

Summary

In this first chapter, I have shown you that you don't have to make a choice between making a profit and doing good. Through your spending, investing, donating and, ultimately, the legacy you leave behind, you can find ways to make a far greater impact than you might ever have thought possible. When they can see the possibilities, people get excited about giving.

---

5 K Thomson, 'Top 7 mistakes Canadians make when donating to charity: Part III', *Your Guide to Charitable Giving and Estate Planning*, www.philanthropymatters.ca/_files/ugd/cbb4e5_343deba5377c4c3ca0632a5aa79d3433.pdf, accessed 25 November 2022

Mindful Money Management puts you in control. People who are mindful with their money make a difference, leaving more to their families, more to charity and less to the tax man. Think twice about the way you spend, invest and donate to vote for your values.

2
Ways In Which The Financial Planning Industry Is Failing You

I often hear stories about the financial planning industry failing to properly serve families. When I met Fred and Marnie, their entire investment portfolio had been sitting in cash, earning nothing for over five years. They didn't have a plan. They were overwhelmed by language and choices they didn't understand. No one had bothered to take the time to explain even the simplest concepts or talk to them about what they could do, or could think about doing in the future. Because no one could be bothered to do this, Fred and Marnie ended up afraid of the future.

They are not alone. Sadly, their story is all too familiar. My colleagues and I hear variations of it all the time. Don't be surprised or embarrassed if you feel like the traditional financial planning industry is not answering your questions or meeting your needs. It's possible that your current strategy and/or advisor is failing you in several ways, ignoring your overall mindset and your deeper needs.

In this chapter I'll talk you through some of the ways in which people can be let down by traditional financial planning that doesn't consider them as a person with values and goals beyond increasing their wealth.

Stealing your peace of mind

Marnie was afraid that she and Fred would outlive their money. This is a common and valid concern. There are plenty of stories out there about people who have worked their whole life preparing for their 'golden years' only to see their hopes and dreams disappear before their eyes once they get there. It's perfectly natural to worry about money and to want to do something to alleviate that fear. That's why Marnie went to see a financial advisor. It's why most of my clients come to see me. People want peace of mind about their future; their financial wellbeing is a large part of that. But Fred and Marnie's advisor didn't give them peace of mind. Quite the opposite. He left them feeling scared, confused and convinced that their future was destined to be a disaster.

Their advisor did not show Fred and Marnie what their money could do in a way that they could understand and appreciate. No one showed them, in clear terms, that they could enjoy a long life and have enough money to provide for a comfortable lifestyle. They *could* enjoy their golden years. They had no reason to worry about their bank balance and could go back to worrying about their sports team. They wanted peace of mind – it was there for the taking.

Ignoring your values

I took some time to talk with Fred and Marnie about what was important to them. What an interesting, novel idea – and certainly, the right place to start. It turned out, Fred and Marnie wanted investments that were kind to the earth. They wanted to support green energy. They had goals of contributing to the university that Fred had attended, his alma mater. And they wanted to establish investments that could cover their grandchildren's educations.

That was a clear set of goals. Easy to understand and just as easy to action. There was nothing particularly out of the ordinary here. But their previous advisor hadn't helped them clarify their values or purpose. He hadn't taken the time to find out what they wanted to do with their money so that he could help them get there. This is a problem I see far too often, and it doesn't need to be that way. For me, this is the obvious starting point. Everything else flows from values and purpose.

Fred and Marnie hadn't been given the opportunity to talk about their 'why', so they lacked the motivation to take the first step. But that's not their job. It's the job of the advisor to understand what their client is striving for so that they can work together to achieve it. They weren't shown how they could make a difference to the lives of the people and the organizations they cared about, and because of that they didn't have a financial plan that would work for them.

Oftentimes, we have this vague thought that someday, maybe, we'll do something – a shadowy, ambiguous thought. Far too often, it never becomes more than that. Your role is to dream about your contribution, to create your perfect scenario. Find your longing and seek out your dream. When you can identify your purpose, your 'why', this will guide and motivate you. It's a light that illuminates the right path in every decision. It works for you because you've built it yourself, based on your needs and your aspirations.

The role of a financial advisor is to understand your motivation so that they can help you achieve your goals and fulfill your purpose. It's not hard to do, but it's not what Fred and Marnie received. It's no wonder that they had trouble getting their investments to align with their values. The question never came up. They weren't given the opportunity to even consider it. Few people are given the opportunity to dream about, seek out and plan for what they want.

Dustyn Lanz, former CEO of the Responsible Investment Association, says that ESG investment is 'still a drop in the bucket', as a result of 'investor inertia' combined with 'advisor inertia', whereby, 'Leading advisors are doing ESG training and talking to clients about responsible investments, but most still aren't.'[6]

Not explaining all your options

Fred and Marnie were not aware that they could choose investments that reflected their values. It was never presented as an option, or even a topic for discussion. They had suggested to their previous advisor that they wanted their investments to avoid certain industries that weren't aligned with their values, but their advisor wouldn't listen. He was only interested in their net worth and investing their money the way he saw fit. He had a plan and wasn't interested in changing it to accommodate the interests of his clients – the people he was supposedly working for.

Let me be clear: you should always be fully advised of *all* your options. In the early stages, there might be additional work involved in finding the financial tools and investment

---

6   D Lanz, 'Successes, challenges and next steps in responsible investing', *Investment Executive* (9 November 2021), www.investmentexecutive.com/inside-track_/dustyn-lanz/successes-challenges-and-next-steps-in-responsible-investing, accessed 18 December 2022

vehicles you're comfortable with, as we talked about in the last chapter, but when you get there, you will find that there are plenty of opportunities to make investments that satisfy your moral compass and meet your specific needs. The range of investment options are practically endless. You just need to go looking, though you'll need some help knowing where, especially in the beginning.

Sometimes, advisors force quick and lazy decisions, skipping over the different options to narrow your choices, limiting you to the solutions they can provide from within their silo. The best way to limit your options and avoid having to explore a more complex or time-consuming plan is to never mention them in the first place.

Silos

It might be my farming background coming out here, but I see no place for isolated silos in financial planning. Think about what a silo is for. A silo is sealed. Air does not flow in and out of a silo. That's perfect if you're storing grain, but in business, creating silos keeps us from seeing all of our options, which leads to lost opportunities. By staying inside a silo, you miss out on all the other options and solutions that are out there. Instead, you should be outside looking to the horizons.

Unfortunately, the financial industry is intentionally structured as a series of silos, and guess who is controlling the doors, deciding who comes in and out and when? Financial planners generally fit into one of three categories:

1. Bank personnel who offer mortgages, loans and investments. They want all your problems solved within the bank's silo.

2. Insurance agents. They want all your problems solved using products in the insurance silo. What could be safer than that?

3. Finally, there are stockbrokers, tasked with growing your portfolio by trading stocks. They want to solve all of your problems through a single-minded focus on the return on your investments.

None of these three will encourage you to look at what's happening in the other silos, but I'll let you in on a little secret – most of them will use the other silos for their own planning. A well-rounded portfolio, whether it's socially responsible or not, needs to draw on the expertise available in each category or silo.

To design your estate, you will also need to consider whether you need the expertise of an accountant and/or an estate lawyer – two further self-contained silos that provide little to no information about the creative options that could help you to accomplish your objectives. Your plan will be most successful when you bring your vision together with the expertise available within varied silos.

Creating unnecessary complexity

I've heard it said that the reason Canadians don't create impactful financial and estate plans is that they don't like to talk about money. But that's not been my experience with the Canadians I speak to. They don't hate talking about money; they hate having conversations about money that leave them feeling confused, intimidated and embarrassed. I mean, who wouldn't?

Have you noticed how many advisors talk in jargon? Sometimes it seems like there's more jargon in financial services than in any other industry. Heck, going to the bank can be worse than going to buy a new cell phone or laptop. 'It's almost like they don't want you to understand,' Fred had commented. When people are confused, guess what they do? They freeze up and do nothing. It was this frozen state that I found Fred and Marnie in. I helped them to thaw out and get started.

I have met many people who don't have plans for their estate or even their retirement. These stages of life are too important to leave to chance. Deep down, they know this, and so do you. But people avoid making decisions because the industry is overwhelming and apathetic. They make it so much easier for people to play the game their way, or not play at all. But do you want to be a spectator on the sidelines of your life and legacy?

As my friend and colleague Betty-Anne Howard wrote in a guest blog for me, 'We need to find ways to make the information we provide to our clients accessible, interesting, relevant and sometimes even enjoyable, given how tedious and inaccessible it's been made by more traditional financial advisors.'[7]

Ignoring you in your growth stages

Financial advisors are picky about who they work with. They want to work with people with more assets and larger asset bases. There's a reason for that. Compliance and related issues make it difficult and expensive to run a financial advisory business. Clients with more assets can generally pay more per hour than those with less. As such, it's pretty easy to get help once you hit a certain asset threshold. Before that, you will find it difficult to get advisors to make time for you. Because of this, many people don't get the help they need in the 'building' phase of their lives and so can make expensive mistakes that could have been avoided, just because they don't know any better.

If you are at a stage of your financial journey where it is easy to find a financial advisor

---

[7] B-A Howard, 'Donating to charity in your will', Mindful Money Management Guest Blog (5 October 2021), https://mindfulmoneymanagement.ca/guest-blog-donating-to-charity-in-your-will-5-ways-to-change-your-world-and-make-a-difference, accessed 16 November 2022

who will take your business, you can help your children and other family members learn about finances and reach their goals. You might also be able to find an advisor who will accept your family members as clients in the growth stages of their financial lives.

Failing to provide value

The way financial advisors and investment managers get paid often gets a lot of attention and there are various models used. We don't need a long discussion about this. Frankly, the discussion itself often becomes another source of confusion and obfuscation. The fee that managers and advisors get for helping you is only an issue in the absence of value. The only number that should matter to you is the return you receive for the fees you pay, and the most important thing to worry about is whether you are receiving advice that enables you to reach your goals, financial and personal. That being said, your advisor should be happy to explain how they get paid and to have this discussion regularly if needed. The best-case scenario is the one where everyone benefits.

Summary

In this chapter, we've looked at the various ways in which the traditional financial services industry is failing people – by preventing you from getting peace of mind, ignoring your values, not explaining all your options, working in silos, creating unnecessary complexity, not being interested in clients who are in their growth stage and failing to provide value. You may have been affected by any or all of these failures.

Think about the times you have engaged with the financial industry. Did you get the sense that your values were the main focus of the possibilities offered to you? Did you receive clear explanations in language you could understand that made your decisions easy? Were you offered non-proprietary options tailor-made to match your goals? Did the advice you received cover multiple silos?

If you do not feel sure of the answer to even one of these questions, the industry has failed to protect your most important asset: your peace of mind. Giving you peace of mind is the primary aim of Mindful Money Management. We'll get into that in the chapters to come.

3
Seven Steps To A Legacy Of Love

There's a story about a nineteenth century Swedish chemist who became one of the wealthiest men in the world. He achieved his wealth by inventing dynamite. Then one day, in Paris, he had a bit of a surprise (to put it mildly). While sitting down to sip his espresso and nibble a croissant, he took a glance at the morning newspaper. The headline on the front page declared that 'The Merchant of Death is dead'. The story described how this Swedish chemist had grown rich by finding ways to kill more people, faster than ever before – and now he was dead.

But the French newspaper had one teeny weeny fact wrong. He wasn't dead. It was his brother who had died. The 'Merchant of Death' was alive and well, but he had lost his brother. This man had the fascinating experience of reading his own obituary, of discovering his legacy. And it was not the legacy he wanted to leave, so he changed it.

Despite inventing dynamite, Alfred Nobel is much better known for the awards he founded using the proceeds of his estate, recognizing those who have made the greatest contributions to humanity across many different fields, including the pursuit and/or promotion of peace. When he died in 1896, with just a handwritten will, Alfred Nobel secured his legacy. He changed the way he would be remembered, from a war profiteer to a philanthropist. He used his will to express his real values.[8]

Wouldn't it be interesting to know what people would say about you? If you read your obituary now, would you be OK with what it said? Or would you respond the way Alfred Nobel

---

[8] E Andrews, 'Did a premature obituary inspire the Nobel Prize?', History (9 December 2016), www.history.com/news/did-a-premature-obituary-inspire-the-nobel-prize, accessed 18 December 2022

did and want to change your legacy? Wouldn't it be nice to think that if you could listen to your eulogy, you would hear words that truly reflected your values? There's still time to look back over your story so far and create, or change, the legacy you'll leave behind.

Legacy is driven by who and what you love. If you're intentional about the legacy you want to leave, the way you protect your family and the causes you care about will become its foundation. But how do you design your contribution? What is your powerful purpose? Through my program, Mindful Money Management, I developed a seven-step process to help you design the contribution you want to leave behind.

7 Steps To A Legacy of Love

Design a Contribution with a Powerful Purpose

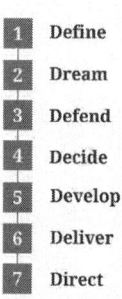

1. Define
2. Dream
3. Defend
4. Decide
5. Develop
6. Deliver
7. Direct

Seven steps to a legacy of love

This process provides you with the keys to unlock the benefits of Mindful Money Management and create a legacy based on the powerful purpose that you identify for yourself.

Step One: Define

When I first met Doris (at least, we'll call her Doris) it became clear that the desire to protect her family was a key driving force in her life. As we worked through the Define step, she told me a secret she'd never shared with her family: when she was nine, her father was stricken with pneumonia and could no longer work. His pay stopped coming in, but the bills didn't. In order to survive, Doris's family had to rely on charity and the kindness of their community.

You can imagine, or perhaps know, how difficult it is to rely on others to meet your basic needs. We all go through life being told that we need to be able to take care of ourselves and our family, and if we can't, we're a failure. Right? Well, no. Life has a way of throwing curveballs at us that we can never fully prepare for. It's not anyone's fault, and in hard times, charity can help. It was because of charity that Doris's family survived, and she wanted to return that support – this was how she defined wealth.

The first step in designing your legacy is to define what wealth means to you. What is important to you? How well do you know yourself? Can you identify exactly what motivates you? What powerful purpose drives you forward? What values can you judge every decision against? Your values are what will motivate you to take the next step. Your core beliefs have been shaped by your family and your community; they come from things you have learned both through example and through study. They are the lens through which you view the world and determine your actions.

You may want to take some time now to complete the 'What's most important in life' exercise to identify your core values. It's intended to focus your thinking and is located with the other resources at the end of the book. You can also find the exercise at https://mindfulmoneymanagement.ca/resources/core-values

By working out what's important in your life, you'll have knowledge of yourself that will better prepare you for the steps that follow.

Step Two: Dream

Doris dreamed. She dreamed of being able to leave money to help her family, especially her grandchildren. She dreamed also of being able to make a contribution that would help people who were going through a tough time, as she and her family had.

The Dream step is where you imagine the life you want to live, where you think about the future you want for yourself and your family and dream about the impact of your life, which you hope will last for generations to come.

In some senses, you are dreaming of the ending, so that you can begin. Steven Covey advises beginning with the end in mind.[9] He is giving business advice but it's also applicable to legacy planning. He talks about the creative process happening twice: first, when you imagine it, and then again when you make it a reality.

---

9 S Covey, *The 7 Habits of Highly Effective People* (Simon and Schuster, 1989)

When planning your impact, think: if you could do anything right now and knew you could not fail, what would you do? If you could change one thing in the world, what would you change? If you could help someone, anyone, who would you help and how? Dream about what you want for your family and about what you want for yourself.

You need to know where you want to end up before you can start the journey. You can create a longer-lasting and more powerful legacy than you may have imagined previously, but first you have to take the time and the energy to dream of it.

Step Three: Defend

Once you have a dream, a plan, defend it. Protect your peace of mind and your impact by stress-testing your plan and modelling different scenarios. The numbers won't lie. You just need to ask the questions. Let's return to Doris as our example.

Doris had a large enough portfolio that she should have felt secure and confident about her ability to support herself throughout her golden years. Even so, Doris was afraid that she would run out of money. Specifically, she was afraid that healthcare needs would erode her savings. She was afraid that her family could have needs that she wouldn't be able to help with. She was afraid that she'd make a mistake and a market downturn would leave her destitute. I suggested that we defend her against that mental toll by stress-testing her portfolio.

Doris, like so many people, thought that a retirement and estate plan was just about money, when in fact it needs to take into consideration so much more: your health, your family's needs, having fun, volunteering and charitable giving. You need to set up your income in the most advantageous way to protect yourself and your loved ones. That involves making decisions about government benefits, workplace pensions, personal savings and how these can all fit together to support your lifestyle, as well as the tax implications of each decision. Proper planning gives you a worry-free retirement and creates a smooth transfer of your assets when you die. That is a gift to your family.

I explained to Doris that defending her plan by stress-testing it meant identifying all of her fears and exploring what it would mean for her plan if they came true, modelling everything mathematically. In the Mindful Money Management process, I call these 'What if?' scenarios. What if she had an unforeseen medical need? What if her family needed her help? What if the markets crashed?

As I modelled each of these situations, and we decided what we would do in each circumstance, Doris grew more confident. She could finally stop worrying. Too often I see folks like Doris worrying about things that they *are* financially prepared for, they just don't know it. They are worrying unnecessarily because no one in the industry has shown them the reality of their financial situation and what this means for them.

Step Four: Decide

Considering all of your options as determined through modelling, it's time to make some decisions.

One of the organizations that had helped Doris's family was the local food bank. Though it was difficult initially, after a few friendly visits they recognized that using the food bank didn't rob them of their dignity, it preserved it. It was a helping hand during a time of need. Doris never forgot that. Now that she was in a position to give back, she wanted to protect that dignity for someone else. Our plan showed Doris how her assets could flow smoothly to her children and grandchildren and still allow her to have a significant impact at the food bank.

Step Five: Develop

Write a blueprint. Thoughts can be random and disorganized for now, it's just important to get them down on paper. When we write things down, we are forced to focus and so can be extra clear on our values and what's most important. It's a matter of getting the ideas out of your head and putting them down where you can see them. From there, you can develop a plan of action, armed with which you can move on to the next step.

Step Six: Deliver

Deliver the message about the decisions and the plan you've made to your beneficiaries. Share your ideas and dreams with them. In doing so, your values will be made clear to your family. Avoid the stress of uncertainly and get everyone involved. You'll appreciate it and so will your family.

Some people are far more worried about this step than they are anything else, and yet it often goes much better than they expect. Be brave. It won't be that bad. More than likely, it will end up being the step you look back on and appreciate the most.

When Doris decided to tell her family what she was planning to do, and why, she organized a family meeting. It was the first time any of them had heard about the hard times she'd faced as a child, and it was emotional for everyone. Her family were happy that she was able to support the food bank, especially after hearing her story. It was an added bonus that it decreased her tax responsibility and increased their inheritance.

By sharing her story and her plan, Doris was able to share the process of designing her legacy, and everyone benefitted from that – emotionally and financially. This is the whole point of Mindful Money Management.

Step Seven: Direct

If and when you have a team of professional advisors to execute your plan, you may find you need help from a specialist with the knowledge and skills to clearly communicate your wishes to your financial advisor, lawyer or accountant. Depending on your situation, you may need them to redirect your assets to fit with your plan. You may need to instruct your specialist to execute, monitor and tweak your plan over time so that it continues to meet the needs you have defined, decided upon and developed throughout the seven steps.

Summary

In this chapter, we've talked about what kind of legacy we hope to leave behind and how we don't have to just hope for it – we can do something now to ensure what we leave after we die is something we can be proud of and that reflects our values. I introduced the Seven Steps to a Legacy of Love, which you can use to unlock the benefits of Mindful Money Management. By designing your legacy, you can be sure it will express your powerful purpose.

4
An Impactful Estate Plan

For many, wealth equals net worth. It's all about the money, all about the numbers. The story ends there. True wealth starts with knowing your values and your purpose. Then you apply sound financial principles to help you live in better accordance with those and to continue to uphold them after you pass, in your legacy. This is the path to true happiness and true wealth.

An impactful estate plan is designed specifically for you, with your purposeful input. This will take some effort, but you'll appreciate and probably even enjoy the journey. I have helped so many clients make this journey; they often start out skeptical and end up impressed and elated. An impactful estate plan is not an off-the-rack plan. It must start with your 'why' and be yours by design. You are like a clothing designer creating a one-of-a-kind collection just for you.

Betty-Anne Howard, a financial planner who, like me, works with people who want to make a positive difference in the world, has identified several significant problems that people encounter when trying to create an impactful estate plan. It starts with the myth that people must choose between supporting their family and giving to charity. Betty-Anne blames the financial services industry for perpetuating this idea and not showing people how to do things differently.

'What is required is a holistic view of your assets, examining the tax implications at your or your surviving spouse's death while exploring how a charitable gift could minimize or even eliminate those taxes,' Betty-Anne explained in a guest blog for Mindful Money Management.[10] 'This takes time, energy and

---

[10] B-A Howard, 'Donating to charity in your will', Mindful Money Management Guest Blog (5 October 2021), https://mindfulmoneymanagement.ca/guest-blog-donating-to-charity-in-your-will-5-ways-to-change-your-world-and-make-a-difference, accessed 16 November 2022

a level of expertise and knowledge that only certain types of financial planners have.' This is something we'll talk more about later.

Betty-Anne told me about something that had happened to one of the charities she works with. They had a donor who wanted to make a contribution. The donor and the charity discussed in detail what the donor wanted done with their gift, but when they mentioned it to their financial advisor, they were told not to do it. Many financial planners just don't do philanthropic planning and won't support your decision to make a gift of your assets. As such, your first goal may be to find a financial planner who understands how to incorporate charitable giving into your estate plan. It takes some looking, but you can do it, and you'll be happy that you did.

This financial planner was wrong to refuse the donor's request, but why did they do it? Betty-Anne explains it this way: 'Most financial advisors are paid via your investments, so any discussion about charitable gifts sends up a red flag, as this could result in fewer assets/ investments to manage.' If you get this kind of reaction from your financial advisor, dig a little deeper into the 'don't do it' response and ask why they are saying this. You have a right to know and understand the rationale behind any and all recommendations they are giving you.

Betty-Anne echoed the message of Mindful Money Management when she highlighted that, 'More and more people, especially as we age, want to have enhanced meaning in our lives, as we question what impact we've had on our children, our families and the world at large. Making a donation or gift in our will is a meaningful and impactful way to do that.'

Betty-Anne and I agree that there is immense pleasure to be found in exploring, planning for and working toward one's legacy and values and the impact you strive to have. It's a personal journey that gives your life significant meaning.

Purpose

I am driven by my belief that we have a responsibility to use our financial resources for the good of ourselves, our families and our society. This purpose drives me to do what I do and help others create an impactful estate plan that reflects their true values. Thinking through Mindful Money Management, talking about it with my clients and chatting on my radio show with others who share my values has been fuelling my professional commitment for many years now. I can think of little else I would rather be doing. (Centre Court at Wimbledon is probably behind me.)

As I've mentioned, purpose stems from values. Values are deeply held beliefs. They are shaped by our family and our community and go back to our childhood and upbringing – possibly even further. People from different faiths, cultures and backgrounds may share the same core values. I remember a discussion in high school with a teacher who asked why he, as an atheist, might encourage his children to attend church or a faith-based school. I answered with clear conviction that an atheist could hold the same values as those taught in a religious institution. Thinking and acting morally can happen within any context – faith-based (and any faith, at that) or not. I've met many people who express similar values to my own, even though our backgrounds couldn't be more different. The conversations I have with these people are often the most interesting.

In 2016 I was selling tickets for our Lions Club fundraiser at the Ancaster Fair. The weather was dreadful and hardly anyone came to the fair that day. With nothing much else to do, I spent hours talking to the young indigenous man in the next booth who was selling beautiful soapstone carvings. It was a deep and meaningful conversation – no small talk that day. As we got further into our conversation, we got deeper into our reasons for being – our purposes in life. We were both intrigued by how much they overlapped. 'So many people talk about their "rights",' I remember him saying. 'In indigenous teaching, we have obligations.' He told me that he chose to follow the teachings he was raised with by fulfilling what he had identified as his deepest obligation: to serve others. This was his driving purpose.

I was fascinated by this definition of personal purpose and meaning. It beautifully described what I am striving for and hoping to do with Mindful Money Management. While some might expect that our cultural and ethnic differences would be a barrier between us, I could clearly see that by having an open and real conversation with the person in front of me, I could find a common ground that was far more compelling than the things that would seem to separate us.

Your purpose in life can and should be expressed through the way you spend, invest and donate. Beyond that, it can continue to be expressed through your legacy. A purpose-driven estate plan can achieve this for you.

Personal history

When I talk about values, I can't help but think about my grandparents. My paternal grandparents were cash crop farmers, and my maternal grandparents were dairy farmers. They shared values that revolved around the farming lifestyle. This included a strong work ethic, connection to the earth and a deep respect for animals. Those themes remain present in my life to this day.

Grandma also gave me my love for books; she always left them laying around for me to read. I remember picking one up from her coffee table; it was called *In Quest of the Least Coin*.[11] As I remember, the book opens with a retelling of a biblical parable. A rich landowner came

---

11 GN Fletcher, *In Quest of the Least Coin: A personal report on a shining example of international giving* (William Morrow & Company Inc, 1968)

into a temple and, with great fanfare, gave large sums of money from his excess. There was also a poor widow who gave only a few coins, but at great personal sacrifice. It was clear to me who the hero in this story was.

Another lesson my grandmother shared with me was the *Parable of the Talents*. As she told it, a rich landowner was preparing to leave on a long trip, leaving his property in the hands of his servants. One servant received five talents, the second received two and the third received one. When the landowner returned from his trip, he evaluated how wise each of them had been in handling his property. The servant who was given five talents had invested them and earned five more. The one who was given two talents likewise increased that to four. But the servant given just one talent had buried it to keep it safe, for fear of losing it. If you are familiar with this story, you will know that the landowner was pleased with the servants who had grown their talents and displeased with the one who acted out of fear, choosing not to do anything with his talent.

These two parables contain many messages, but what they taught me most is that our generosity is not measured by how much we give but by what it means for us to give it. That says something about who we are.

We all have something to give. The second of the parables above taught me that we all have 'talents' to offer the world. Our responsibility – to ourselves and to everyone around us – is to nurture those talents and put them to use. To do anything less is the greatest waste imaginable.

Your 'why'

If you are not sure where to begin looking for your 'why', I suggest you start with your family and community. This is where the 'why' is for nine out of ten people who walk through my door. Let me give you a few examples.

My friend Joan is leaving a gift in her will for a highly personal reason. When Joan was young, her sister died; she struggled emotionally and found it hard to deal with the loss. Because of her experience as a child, she enthusiastically gives her time and money to organizations that support children's mental health. That's her 'why'. Joan does what she does because of a love of family.

Luke was paralyzed with grief after the death of his wife, Lucille. He couldn't continue in his own career for some time. Because of her careful planning, Lucille was able to protect Luke. No doubt she knew how he would initially deal with her death and did what she could to help. Lucille's life insurance and pension gave Luke the time he needed to grieve. Though he no longer has her daily physical company, he still feels her caring and comforting presence in his life. He told me, 'I think Lucy set this up so that I'd have more time to talk to her.' Now Luke wants to create a legacy in his wife's memory by doing the same for someone else. I am guiding Luke through the process, helping him to create a substantial charitable legacy in Lucille's name, while still protecting their children's inheritance.

As a young man, Stan suffered a debilitating stroke and spent eighteen months in rehab, what seemed like forever for a man of his age. Stan was grateful for the support of the nurses and healthcare workers who helped him in his fight back to health during that challenging time. After he had recovered, the rehab centre became Stan's community. He has worked tirelessly as a volunteer and has helped to raise money for the centre. Whenever they need his help, he is there ready to lend a hand.

Joan's focus on children's mental health, Luke's desire to create a legacy in Lucille's name and Stan's commitment to helping his rehab centre community, are their driving forces. Love of family and care for community inspire the 'why' for each of them. Their drive inspires me to ensure each of them is able to make the difference they hope to see in the world.

See identifying your 'why' as an opportunity to share. We each have a unique way of looking at the world. It is essential that you share that view with your family and your wider community. There are many ways to share your vision with the world, both today and in the years to come.

The right team and leadership

Creating a designed contribution requires that you have the right team offering you exemplary leadership and their full support. Not recognizing the need for a team is a big mistake and, because it happens right at the start of your journey, it can have an impact all the way through the process. It's like extending your house. You don't know where to start. You need a general contractor, someone who is able and willing to see your vision through to its conclusion. It is still you who makes all the decisions; it is the contractor's job to lay out all the options in a way you understand. They work alongside an architect, who will take your ideas plus the contractor's expertise and draw up a blueprint. The general contractor will also speak to the plumber, the carpenter, the drywaller and the electricians. This is invaluable, because it's unlikely that you have the expertise to interpret the blueprints and communicate with the various trades; it's like speaking another language. Your general contractor makes sure the plumber, electrician and all the other tradesmen on site speak to each other to align schedules and provide access; they facilitate communication between those silos.

In financial services, there are generally several kinds of planners and advisors, each in their own silo, each of them all with their own biases. Then we have accountants and lawyers, who speak their own languages. What there often isn't, though, is a general contractor to aid communication between silos and move the project forward. In this way, the industry is failing you.

Who in your financial team is playing the role of general contractor? Is there a person who can speak the language of all the different people you need? Who understands your vision and can communicate that to other involved parties? Who can oversee the execution of your plan?

In terms of estate planning, you want an estate planning specialist to act as your 'general contractor'. This will enable you to make some progress. Returning to Betty-Anne's story, remember the advice about asking a financial advisor why they don't want you to make a particular provision in your will? 'Sometimes it's simply a matter of the financial advisor gaining a better understanding of what you want to accomplish,' she explains. 'Seek out the information you need to understand your options and the advantages and disadvantages of different charitable giving strategies.'[12]

---

12 B-A Howard, 'Donating to charity in your will', Mindful Money Management Guest Blog (5 October 2021), https://mindfulmoneymanagement.ca/guest-blog-donating-to-charity-in-your-will-5-ways-to-change-your-world-and-make-a-difference, accessed 16 November 2022

Sometimes, though, it takes more than doing your research and explaining your wishes to an advisor who is not used to thinking about financial planning through this lens. I strongly suggest engaging a financial planner specializing in philanthropy to help guide you through this process as they will be able to add immense value and spot opportunities others may not.

Let's take insurance policies as an example, as these are a great way to maximize your gift to a charity. A recent statement from your insurance company should tell you what type of policy you have and how it is structured. If not, you can find out by contacting either the person who sold you the policy or a licensed insurance advisor who can find out on your behalf.

As a specialist in philanthropic giving, Betty-Anne knows that a life insurance policy owned by a charity that is made the beneficiary of that policy can increase what you are able to gift to charity and, therefore, your impact – so long as the policy is structured to do exactly that. However, this is not possible with all types of insurance policy. As Betty-Anne explains, 'There are so many different insurance policies – term, term to age 100, whole life, limited pay, participating/non-participating, some with cash values and some without. Not to mention how difficult it can be to figure out the exact type of insurance policy you need.'

I can't stress enough the need for specialists who know the ins and outs of impactful estate planning. The same advisor who helped you in the accumulation phase of your financial life may not be the most appropriate when it comes to thinking about your retirement income. They may also lack the expertise to help you design your legacy. We're talking about a different paradigm here, one that requires an extensive, detailed knowledge in a specific area and a different skill set. This might sound like a giant task, but the right advisor with the right array of expertise will put everything straight very quickly.

A work in progress

Over time, your plan will need to be monitored, as it will evolve. Jill and Carol went through the Designed Contribution program with Mindful Money Management ten years ago. At that time, their niece and nephew were just starting out in their adult lives; Grace had recently graduated from college and Jack was engaged and beginning his career. Jill and Carol directed a significant part of their wealth to Grace and Jack to help them get started. In the ten years that followed, Jill and Carol's wealth grew as their small farm and their investments increased in value. Grace and Jack had become well established in their respective careers and weren't in need of as much support, so Jill and Carol decided to increase the percentage of their wealth that was going to charity.

Look back over the past decade. Has your financial plan remained static or has it evolved? To be truly impactful, you need to continually evaluate it to make sure it remains oriented to your circumstances and goals as those change.

Summary

In this chapter, we've talked about what makes an impactful estate plan and how to build one. An impactful estate plan has several defining characteristics. Most importantly, though, it is purpose-driven, driven by a clear goal or mission that propels you to move the process forward. The 'why' of that purpose is personal to you – you have your own reasons for wanting to make a particular kind of impact. An impactful estate plan serves a greater need, one that is often focused on family and community. Your planning is an opportunity to share your values and involve your family in these decisions. It might inspire them in their own philanthropic journey and will give them an understanding of your motivations. This is often a meaningful conversation that can drive your legacy forward in ways you might never have expected.

To deliver your plan, you need the right leader, leading the right team. The plan is a work in progress and you need to find your general contractor to get this thing going.

5
Choice

George and Margaret were confused. They felt there were too many options when it came to deciding how to set up their estate plan. George was especially frustrated because he didn't know where to start. I began by reminding them to think in terms of what they wanted to accomplish; to begin with the end in mind. We started by completing the values exercise and talked about their life story, their experiences and family background. As simple as it sounds, this is almost always where I start. It's always a lot of fun for both the client and me.

As simple as ABC

George and Margaret had two daughters, Ruth Anne and Mary Kate. The younger of the two, Mary Kate, was born with Down's syndrome. Mary Kate's passion is swimming, and she frequently wins awards at the Special Olympics, with her whole family cheering her on. George and Margaret wanted to strike a balance between helping their two daughters and leaving a gift for the Special Olympics. They had three possible beneficiaries of their estate: Revenue Canada, their family and their preferred charity. With planning, they could choose just two of these.

I presented them with three possible courses of action, options A, B and C:

- **A**lready decided. Option A is the best plan for the tax man. If you decide not to make a plan, the government will make one for you.

- **B**etter for your family. You can plan to mitigate taxes and increase your estate to benefit your family.

- **C**onsider your legacy. You can redirect taxes to a charitable cause that you care about.

Let's look at these three options in more detail.

A: Already decided

Without any other plan in place, in Canada the government will take half, or more, of your registered assets. Putting ourselves in George's and Margaret's shoes, they are both sixty years old and have $600,000 in registered assets. If they do no planning, they will have $700,000 in registered assets if they have both died by eighty-four. The taxes owed on their registered assets would be $350,000 and their family would receive the remaining $350,000.

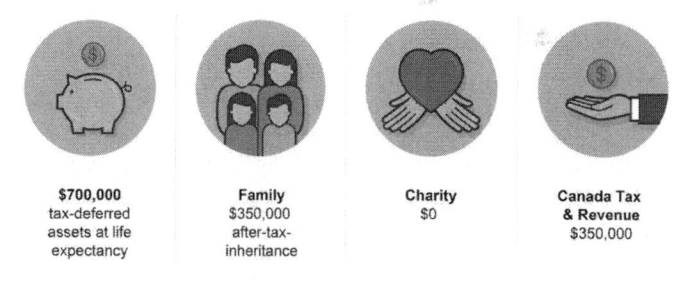

$700,000
tax-deferred assets at life expectancy

Family
$350,000
after-tax-inheritance

Charity
$0

Canada Tax & Revenue
$350,000

Option A: Already decided

B: Better for your family

If George and Margaret do some redirecting, they could have registered assets of $500,000 at life expectancy. In this scenario, the taxes owed upon their deaths would be $250,000 and their family would receive $750,000.

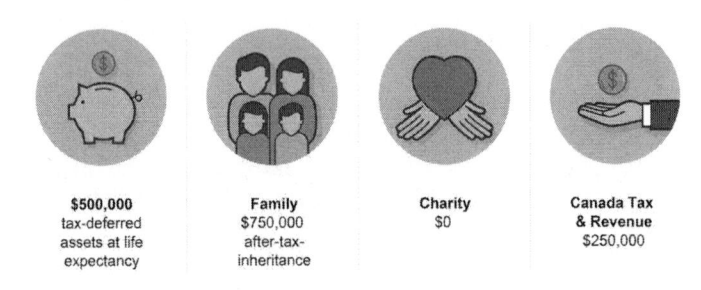

| $500,000 tax-deferred assets at life expectancy | Family $750,000 after-tax-inheritance | Charity $0 | Canada Tax & Revenue $250,000 |

Option B: Better for your family

C: Consider your legacy

Anyone can choose to redirect taxes to a charitable cause that is meaningful to them. If George and Margaret choose to include a charity in their estate planning, they could eliminate tax altogether. They could give $500,000 to charity and their family's inheritance would be $500,000. Their family is still receiving $150,000 more than in option A.

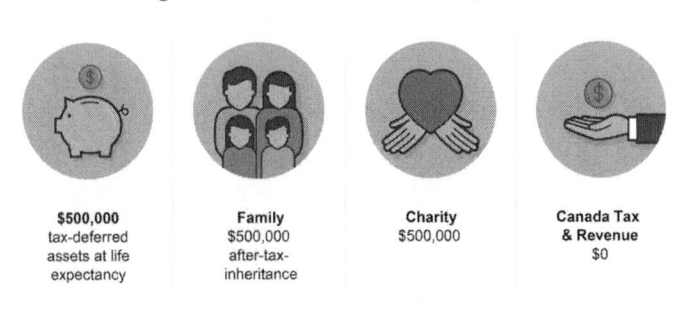

| $500,000 tax-deferred assets at life expectancy | Family $500,000 after-tax-inheritance | Charity $500,000 | Canada Tax & Revenue $0 |

Option C: Consider your legacy

CHOICE

The three options I have presented above, and that I shared with Margaret and George, involve the use of multiple silos within financial planning. This is why you need a specialist to oversee your estate planning. In option B, we redirect some of our couple's assets from the bank (banking silo) to a life insurance policy (insurance silo) over a period of twenty years. This has the effect of moving those assets from a taxable position to a tax-free position.

In option C, we do the same repositioning into the same life insurance policy, which pays out $500,000 (the registered assets) tax-free to the beneficiaries, which in this scenario is the couple's favourite charity. This creates a tax credit that eliminates the taxes owing.

When we considered their registered assets, it became apparent that the best solution for George and Margaret was option B. I then showed them how they could still pursue their goal of providing for the Special Olympics using another underutilized strategy available to Canadians.

What and *how* you give matters. As part of their portfolio, George and Margaret held a stock (another silo) outside of their Registered Retirement Savings Plan (RSP) or Registered Retirement Income Fund (RIF) that had appreciated in value over the years. They were reluctant to sell the stock because of the capital gains tax that would be triggered. I explained to them that tax legislation would allow them to give those stocks to charity in kind, and that by gifting appreciated securities they would not trigger the capital gains tax and still receive the full charitable tax credit.

By choosing that part of their portfolio to give to charity, they saved twice. This stock had cost them $10,000 twenty-three years previously and was now worth $50,000. The capital gains tax would have cost them $10,000. Instead, they gifted the stock to the Special Olympics. This meant that they did not have to pay the $10,000 capital gains tax and they got a tax credit for the full $50,000 value of the gift, saving them another $25,000 in tax. In total, donating the stock saved them $35,000 in tax and enabled them to make a huge impact in supporting the future of the Special Olympics. George and Margaret were thrilled to be able to present this gift and support the program that had meant so much to their family.

Let's be clear about something: the Canada Revenue Agency is not the villain. Taxes certainly have an impact on your estate, but our tax legislation is generous and offers many strategies to encourage charitable giving. These strategies mean that you don't have to leave half your estate to the government if you don't want to, but they remain largely unknown.

You have a choice. Contrary to the popular saying, 'Nothing is certain except death and taxes', we do have a choice about taxes. Most of us don't plan or choose to leave 50% of our wealth to the government, but that's what will happen if you don't plan.

Voluntary philanthropy makes us feel good. The involuntary philanthropist is the taxpayer, which doesn't seem as joyful. But you have an opportunity; with proper planning ahead of time, you can redirect your taxes to causes you care about. If you would prefer to be a voluntary philanthropist and choose what you contribute to, planning is essential.

Special needs

George and Margaret's estate required another level of planning that isn't the case for many, as they were concerned about providing for Mary Kate after they had gone. People who care for a special needs child, and hope to continue to do so after they have passed, must be sure they are dealing with advisors who are experienced in working with special needs families. They need an advisor who understands the unique considerations these situations bring, such as tax deductions and savings vehicles available to their family while they are alive, as well as the special considerations that need to be applied when creating their will.

My colleague Barry Ames has spent his career supporting families like George and Margaret's and I often go to him for specialist advice. When I interviewed Barry for my radio show and we discussed families and situations like this, he highlighted that, 'One of the most critical areas where I can add value is to remind them of the importance of completing wills and Powers of Attorney.' He said he meets many families where parents haven't done that and don't know who they want to look after their child when they're gone. He strongly encourages them to think about this, make the decision and get it in writing.[13]

There are special provisions that can be put in your will to protect your legacy while ensuring that any provincial benefits that your son or daughter is receiving from the government don't suddenly come to an end simply because there is money available to them from their parents' estate. Unfortunately, this is often overlooked, which creates hardship and confusion.

Barry works with a network of professionals who stay on top of these requirements for people like George and Margaret and their daughter. There are financial planners and lawyers who specialize in helping families with more complicated needs. It is possible that you, or someone you know, may need their help. You can find a valuable guide to tax, benefits, trusts and wills for those with disabilities at https://communitylivingontario.ca/resources/wills-estate-guide.

---

13 L Whetham, 'The joys and responsibilities of complicated kids: Guest Barry Ames CFP® BA', Stepright with Lynn (rebranded Mindful Money Management) (19 March 2014), https://archive.org/details/podcast_stepright-with-lynn-lynn-whe_the-joys-responsibilities_1000379915180, accessed 25 November 2022

Whatever needs your family has, you need advisors who understand your circumstances and priorities and can present your options in clear and simple language so that you can make mindful choices that will move you toward your desired outcomes.

Summary

You have more choice than you might think. The amount of tax you pay is one such choice. If you want to make a positive impact with your legacy, and if you want to support your family while also helping the causes and charities you care about, you can achieve this with the right planning and support from advisors who understand your needs. Whatever your circumstances, there will be multiple options available to you; find an advisor who can present you with *all* the options, so that you can make the choices that are right for you and your family.

6
Mindful Communication

The largest transfer of wealth the world has ever seen will take place over the next few years. A trillion dollars will be transferred from one generation to the next. In many cases, the receivers will not be prepared for this; some families don't even want to talk about it. This is a recipe for trouble.[14]

Families *must* talk about money. Unless you talk about it, people make assumptions, feel

---

14 J Heath, 'Canadian inheritances could hit $1 trillion over the next decade and both bequeathers and beneficiaries need to be ready', *The Financial Post* (8 April 2021), https://tinyurl.com/39bs98xr, accessed 22 March 2022

confused and end up overwhelmed. When these conversations don't happen, the legacy that is left, instead of providing security and contentment, breeds tragedy and heartbreak. Don't let this happen to your family – have the conversation.

Stories abound about people who win the lottery, only to be left penniless just a few years later. These are stories of excessive spending and mindless giving (more like scattering); becoming targets of con artists and swindlers; and devastating descents into substance abuse and personal neglect. Many of the stories end in isolation, divorce and sometimes even death.

You may have come across the term 'affluenza'. Affluenza is the opposite of Mindful Money Management. The term was aptly coined by John de Graaf, who helped popularize the term in the 1990s, to describe 'a painful, contagious, socially transmitted condition of overload, debt, anxiety and waste resulting from the dogged pursuit of more.'[15] The term has even been used as a defence in court, attributing a

---

15 J de Graaf, D Wann and TH Naylor, *Affluenza: How overconsumption is killing us – and how to fight back* (Berrett-Koehler, 2014)

defendant's terrible actions to 'a malady said to result from excessive privilege.'[16]

I agree with Warren Buffett's take on the subject. He says that you should leave your children 'enough money that they would feel they could do anything, but not so much that they could do nothing.'[17]

It could be considered neglectful to leave your wealth to others without teaching them what to do with it. You owe it to them to make the transfer beneficial, not stressful. Make sure your financial legacy is a blessing and not a curse by engaging in mindful communication with all the relevant parties.

Storytelling

How better to communicate your values than by telling your story? Help your family

---

16 M McPhate, 'Use of "Affluenza" didn't begin with Ethan Couch case', *The New York Times* (29 December 2015), www.nytimes.com/2015/12/30/us/use-of-affluenza-didnt-begin-with-ethan-couch-case.html, accessed 22 March 2022

17 RI Kirkland and C Gottlieb, 'Should you leave it all to the children?', *Fortune Magazine* (29 September 1986), https://money.cnn.com/magazines/fortune/fortune_archive/1986/09/29/68098/index.htm, accessed 21 March 2022

understand your legacy, not only in terms of the wealth you leave behind but also the story of the life that preceded and created it. You can begin telling that story, though it is not yet complete while you are still alive.

Often, the only time you see or hear someone talking about their legacy is at the beginning of a whodunnit, with the about-to-be-deceased reading their last will and testament – and you just know something bad is about to happen. Telling your story, though it necessarily touches on your death, doesn't have to be this morbid.

My friend Tom Deans, intergenerational wealth expert and author, says families need to rekindle the art of storytelling. This can help them to have those difficult conversations about money, life and death. Tom was a guest on my radio show, where we talked about this in depth. I'll reproduce some of that conversation below, but it's an episode well worth listening to in full.

TALKING ABOUT MONEY – TOM DEANS[18]

'It's usually at meals shared with family and friends, the people who matter most, where we share stories, and the studies show we're having fewer and fewer meals with our families,' Tom told me. 'In ancient times, we sat around fires and told stories; if you were family, you heard those stories. If you were smart, you listened and you did something with it.' That wisdom, Tom explained, was passed down over generations and throughout the history of civilisations.

This raises the question of why, then, do we need to be reminded to ask questions, have conversations and communicate our thoughts, values and needs? Only when we choose to engage in real, intentional conversations can we have meaningful communication. This is the kind of communication that needs to happen, all the way down through the generations, where everyone is available and able to participate.

On the surface, it seems simple. Yet many of us struggle to properly express our thoughts and feelings about difficult topics like family,

---

18 L Whetham, 'A death built with care: Guest Tom Deans', Stepright with Lynn (rebranded Mindful Money Management) (4 February 2015), www.soundcloud.com/mindfulmoneymanagement/a-death-built-with-care-with-tom-deans, accessed 15 March 2022

aging, money and inheritance. Tom believes some of the awkwardness and procrastination is subconscious.

'There's a lot of superstition wrapped up in this subject,' he pointed out. 'Like, if I write a will, I'm taunting death. And we are, for many, many Canadians, the first generation to actually die with a surplus. It's not that long ago that a will was kind of a luxury.'

Tom says one of the most important stories that you can share with your family is the story of how your family's wealth was created. He was told stories about the risks his grandfather took as a business owner, how his factory burned down and he rebuilt it, which sparked feelings of gratitude for Tom. 'When I inherited some wealth from my grandparents, I was connected to that wealth in a very profound way because of the stories, because I knew how it was created. It was difficult. It was hard. It's never been easy to accumulate wealth in our family,' he said. 'The storytelling connects the generations together and creates a generation of inheritors that have a respect for inherited wealth.'

Tom believes that every adult should have a will and that estate planning is not just for the uber wealthy. For many, it's the only written word they leave behind. 'Not everyone writes books and articles or even love letters. So when they die, they leave the people who matter most in their lives with lots of questions about what they thought was important. A will is more than just a document that says, "You get the lawn mower, you get my watch, you get my cash, and you get the cottage." It can be a document that says, "These are assets that I want everyone to share in, and this is how I want you to share in them."'

Tom advocates for family meetings where time is set aside to discuss wealth and wills, but what if your situation is a difficult one and you can't imagine having those discussions with your family? Not doing so can have 'devastating outcomes', said Tom. If you aren't comfortable doing it alone, having advisors present can help. It can let you concentrate on the emotion while someone else handles the numbers.

He also emphasizes the importance of listening. 'Sit your children down and say, "When we die, here's what we have in mind. But what do you think? What would you do with an inheritance?" It's not about the people with the money necessarily telling people how it's going to be. It's actually listening and being informed by their beneficiaries.' He says most people are relieved that someone else has brought the subject up. 'It's on everyone's mind. Watching parents age, wondering who's going to step up.'

Advisors can provide solutions that have worked for other clients and can take on a trusted role for the whole family. Once it's done, the conversation has been had and plans have been made and communicated to everyone involved, you can get back to living and building the legacy you have agreed on.

Teaching about giving

I asked my friend Anne MacKay, who helps non-profits fundraise to continue their work, how we can talk to children about charitable giving. Anne grew up on a farm. Each summer, they sold the sweetcorn they grew.

'At the end of one summer, my parents said, "We have some money left over, and we'd like to give it to charity. Why don't you each come forward and make a suggestion about where you think it should go?" That was a very empowering thing to do for little kids,' she recalled. 'My brothers and I each brought forward our ideas and made our pitch. I remember thinking, "Wow, I get to have a say in where this money goes!" It was really amazing.'

Anne believes that talking to kids about charitable giving encourages them to start thinking about the world beyond themselves. She suggests asking them questions like, 'If you had $20 to give, who would you give it to? What kinds of things would you want to support?'

Anne suggests that children will give black and white answers. 'You know, all kids should be allowed to go to school and all animals should be safe. For tweens, I might ask, "What kind of charity would have impact for kids your age? Can you do some research and find a charity that can do that?" Then maybe for older kids, I might ask them to interview somebody. "Can you find out where grandma has given to and why? And if somebody was going to interview you when you're her age, what would you say?"'

Many families encourage their children to set a little aside from their allowance and make donations to charity. Why not start a giving tradition with the children in your family? Each family member can begin the Mindful Money Management process for themselves and build a lifetime of conscious decision-making about money. This is the way legacies are built.

Summary

In this chapter, we've talked about how important it is to communicate your values, wishes and plans for your life (and death). It's not always easy, as these are often difficult topics to confront, but communicating your values and wishes is well worth the effort. Why not do it at your next family get together? Whether it's around the fire pit at the cottage, on the roof watching the fireworks, or anywhere else – just make it happen. I promise that you'll be happy you did.

Conclusion

When visiting a friend's cottage in the lovely lakeside community of Grand Bend, I went for an early morning walk down the beach. I could tell that I was not the first to walk there that day because there were already footprints in the sand. The person was no longer there but I still knew things about them. I could tell how big their feet were and what kind of balance they walked with. I could tell that they had walked alone, and would have known if they'd walked with a child or another adult.

It occurred to me that we all leave footprints behind when we leave this world.

These footprints tell those we leave behind something about us and what we stood for. Will your footprint say what you want it to? Heck, will mine? What can each of us do to make sure we make the biggest footprint possible? And that it makes the kind of difference we want it to make?

My goal is to make a difference by helping *you* make a difference. I hope this book will give you a place to start. Your journey has only just begun, but I feel sure it will be a journey that you will be excited to make and share with those you love.

Contribution by design

Mindful Money Management asks you to assign meaning to your financial life. Decisions become easier when you understand their significance. For instance, when you have young children, every decision you make is focused on what is best for them. That framework makes every decision important and its purpose clear.

Let your values guide your financial decisions and find a purpose outside of yourself, whether that be a cause or a person you love.

CONCLUSION

In his book *Driven by Purpose*, my friend and colleague Ryan Fraser says: '… we each need to think about how our actions and our personal values can and should positively impact the people and world around us. This may be the most important legacy question of all, and in many ways, it has nothing to do with money.'[19]

It is beyond the scope of this book to explain every strategy that can be applied to your financial journey. The intention here is simply to encourage you to explore your potential. You have your own story to share, building on what is important to you. It is you who will write the next chapter of your story.

Unique to you are:

- Your motivations
- Your stories and how they shape your desired impact
- Your financial resources and the kinds of assets you hold
- Your special family considerations

---

19 R Fraser, *Driven by Purpose: 32 remarkable stories about growing your wealth and leaving a transformational legacy* (Milner & Associates Inc, 2020)

Some strategies may seem complicated but fortunately, you don't need to be an expert. You do not need to understand the details of every possible strategy and how to apply it to your situation. All you need to do is to work with the right person, one who knows the tax rules and can identify the opportunities that will enable you to make the kind of difference *you* want to make. Someone who understands both your wishes and the financial tools that can help make them come true.

There are many resources available to guide you in creating a designed contribution. I encourage you to seek out the help you need to gain clarity and make your decisions easy.

Keith Thomson, Toronto philanthropist and CEO of The Donor Motivation Program® in Canada, says it's unreasonable to assume we can become experts about everything on top of our own professions and responsibilities. 'When it comes to philanthropy and your legacy goals, hiring an individual who specializes in this discipline is key.' To find that person, he suggests focusing on the three benefits they need to deliver: your peace of mind, a financial plan ensuring an income stream you won't outlive, and building a legacy that

CONCLUSION

leaves a lasting impact, not only now but long after you're gone.[20]

I dream of a future where we all intend to make a difference, to make a mindful, intentional contribution, and where planning for this is commonplace. To this end, I encourage you to talk about death, money and taxes. It's a trio of topics most people avoid but, when you don't shy away and talk about them, when you plan and apply the appropriate expertise, you can give far more.

I hope that after reading this book you know what your next step will be toward creating your contribution by design, but please feel free to reach out if you need more help in identifying or taking that next step.

I want to leave you with one last thought. A little while ago I was going through a box of items that had belonged to my parents. I came across my mother's autograph book. The first entry was my grandfather. If you can make it out, the text in the top right corner says

---

20 K Thomson, 'Top 7 mistakes Canadians make when donating to charity: Part III', *Your Guide to Charitable Giving and Estate Planning*, www.philanthropymatters.ca/_files/ugd/cbb4e5_343deba5377c4c3ca0632a5aa79d3433.pdf, accessed 6 March 2022

Putnam Jan 18, 1943. My mother would have been twelve.

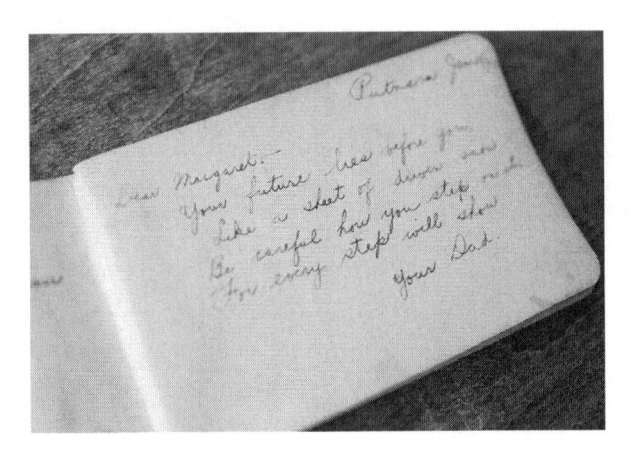

The inscription reads:

> 'Dear Margaret,
>
> Your future lies before you
> Like a sheet of driven snow.
>
> Be careful how you step on it,
> For every step will show.
>
> Your Dad.'

This message, simple and yet profound, seems like an appropriate one to close with. It expresses the intent of Mindful Money Management. My hope is you enjoy many conversations sharing and protecting your personal values and that this ending is your beginning.

Resources

Further reading

TW Deans, *Willing Wisdom: 7 questions successful families ask* (Detente Financial Press, 2014)

TW Deans' book is a must-read for anyone serious about leaving a profound and enduring legacy for their family, friends and community.

K Thomson, *What Was Your Great Grandmother's Name? 50 thoughts on how Canadian philanthropy can transform you, your family and your community* (Keith Thomson, 2011)

Core values exercise

This exercise is designed to help you define what's most important in your life.

Step 1: From the following list, select and highlight between ten and twenty of the values that resonate with you.

Step 2: Begin to group these into some that are similar.

Step 3: You may now have three to five topics. Choose the value within each list that best sums up that topic for you.

Step 4: List these values in order of their importance to you. These are your top three to five values.

Abundance	Acceptance	Accessibility
Accomplishment	Accuracy	Achievement
Acknowledgement	Activeness	Adaptability
Adoration	Adroitness	Adventure
Affection	Affluence	Aggressiveness
Agility	Alertness	Altruism
Ambition	Amusement	Anticipation
Appreciation	Approachability	Articulateness

RESOURCES

Assertiveness	Assurance	Attentiveness
Attractiveness	Audacity	Availability
Awareness	Awe	Balance
Beauty	Being the best	Belonging
Benevolence	Bliss	Boldness
Bravery	Brilliance	Buoyancy
Calmness	Camaraderie	Candour
Capability	Care	Carefulness
Celebrity	Certainty	Challenge
Charity	Charm	Chastity
Cheerfulness	Clarity	Cleanliness
Comfort	Commitment	Compassion
Completion	Composure	Concentration
Confidence	Conformity	Congruency
Connection	Consciousness	Consistency
Contentment	Continuity	Contribution
Control	Conviction	Conviviality
Coolness	Cooperation	Cordiality
Correctness	Courage	Courtesy
Craftiness	Creativity	Credibility
Cunning	Curiosity	Daring
Decisiveness	Decorum	Deference
Delight	Dependability	Depth
Desire	Determination	Devotion
Devoutness	Dexterity	Dignity
Diligence	Direction	Directness
Discipline	Discovery	Discretion
Diversity	Dominance	Dreaming

Drive	Duty	Dynamism
Eagerness	Economy	Ecstasy
Education	Effectiveness	Efficiency
Elation	Elegance	Empathy
Encouragement	Endurance	Energy
Enjoyment	Entertainment	Enthusiasm
Excellence	Excitement	Exhilaration
Expectancy	Expediency	Experience
Expertise	Exploration	Expressiveness
Extravagance	Extroversion	Exuberance
Fairness	Faith	Fame
Family	Fascination	Fashion
Fearlessness	Ferocity	Fidelity
Fierceness	Financial independence	Firmness
Fitness	Flexibility	Flow
Fluency	Focus	Fortitude
Frankness	Freedom	Friendliness
Frugality	Fun	Gallantry
Generosity	Gentility	Giving
Grace	Gratitude	Gregariousness
Growth	Guidance	Happiness
Harmony	Health	Heart
Helpfulness	Heroism	Holiness
Honesty	Honour	Hopefulness
Hospitality	Humility	Humour
Hygiene	Imagination	Impact
Impartiality	Independence	Industry

RESOURCES

Ingenuity	Inquisitiveness	Insightfulness
Inspiration	Integrity	Intelligence
Intensity	Intimacy	Intrepidness
Introversion	Intuition	Intuitiveness
Inventiveness	Investing	Joy
Judiciousness	Justice	Keenness
Kindness	Knowledge	Leadership
Learning	Liberation	Liberty
Liveliness	Logic	Longevity
Love	Loyalty	Majesty
Making a difference	Mastery	Maturity
Meekness	Mellowness	Meticulousness
Mindfulness	Modesty	Motivation
Mysteriousness	Neatness	Nerve
Obedience	Open-mindedness	Openness
Optimism	Order	Organization
Originality	Outlandishness	Outrageousness
Passion	Peace	Perceptiveness
Perfection	Perkiness	Perseverance
Persistence	Persuasiveness	Philanthropy
Piety	Playfulness	Pleasantness
Pleasure	Poise	Polish
Popularity	Potency	Power
Practicality	Pragmatism	Precision
Preparedness	Presence	Privacy
Proactivity	Professionalism	Prosperity
Prudence	Punctuality	Purity

Realism	Reason	Reasonableness
Recognition	Recreation	Refinement
Reflection	Relaxation	Reliability
Religiousness	Resilience	Resolution
Resolve	Resourcefulness	Respect
Rest	Restraint	Reverence
Richness	Rigour	Sacredness
Sacrifice	Sagacity	Saintliness
Sanguinity	Satisfaction	Security
Self-control	Selflessness	Self-reliance
Sensitivity	Sensuality	Serenity
Service	Sexuality	Sharing
Shrewdness	Significance	Silence
Silliness	Simplicity	Sincerity
Skillfulness	Solidarity	Solitude
Soundness	Speed	Spirit
Spirituality	Spontaneity	Stability
Stealth	Stillness	Strength
Structure	Success	Support
Supremacy	Surprise	Sympathy
Synergy	Teamwork	Temperance
Thankfulness	Thoughtfulness	Thrift
Tidiness	Timeliness	Traditionalism
Tranquility	Transcendence	Trust
Trustworthiness	Truth	Understanding
Unflappability	Uniqueness	Unity
Usefulness	Utility	Valour
Variety	Victory	Vigour

RESOURCES

Virtue	Vision	Vitality
Vivacity	Warmth	Watchfulness
Wealth	Wilfulness	Willingness
Winning	Wisdom	Wittiness
Wonder	Youthfulness	Zeal

Acknowledgements

Thank you to Christine Rier and Sherry Grosz, who many years ago set out with me on the mission to let people know that with planning they can make a far bigger difference than they ever imagined.

Thank you to every guest on the Mindful Money Management radio show who helped to shape my thinking.

Thank you to Buddy Brennan and Todd Race for helping to clarify my messages.

Thanks to The Donor Motivation Program® for the opportunity to share this message on a wider scale.

Thanks to Joan Cosby, Joanne Harris-Bedford, Betty-Anne Howard and Tara Tennant for their unwavering support.

Thank you to Rethink Press and the Dent program for making this book a reality.

The Author

Lynn Whetham is a financial writer, educator, speaker and radio show host. As a professor, she specialized in teaching financial planning, assisting people to create a retirement of their own design. Lynn is passionate about helping individuals discover the tools and knowledge they need to maximize their financial and philanthropic opportunities. As a result, Lynn is able to enhance the lives of the people with whom she works by multiplying their impact on those causes that are most meaningful to them.

Lynn is an expert writer for the publication *Neighbours of West Galt*. She has thousands of listeners following her radio show, Mindful Money Management, which is dedicated to empowering socially conscious individuals to manage their financial resources for the benefit of themselves, their families and the greater community. Lynn's first book, *Retire Abundantly*, was published in 2018.

Lynn has served the arts community as a board member of the Kiwanis Boys Choir and, before joining the board of the Grand River Festival, acted as their volunteer co-ordinator. She is currently a Lions Club International member and a past member of the board of The Bridges, the Cambridge Homeless Shelter.

Lynn believes that rural roots help to keep her grounded. She is not afraid of hard work or an active lifestyle. Lynn has four adult daughters and three grandchildren. She lives on a hobby farm with her husband, Neil, where

THE AUTHOR

her favourite pastimes are trail riding with her horse, Winchester, and cuddling with her dog, Newton.

- 🌐 www.mindfulmoneymanagement.ca
- ✉ lynn@mindfulmoneymanagement.ca
- 🔗 www.linkedin.com/in/lynn-whetham-cfp®-3a29b76